fondue

by Robert Carmack

TUTTLE PUBLISHING
Tokyo • Rutland, Vermont • Singapore

Published by Tuttle Publishing, an imprint of Periplus
Editions, with editorial offices at 130 Joo Seng Road,
#06-01, Singapore 368357, and 364 Innovation Drive,
North Clarendon, VT 05759, USA.

Hardcover ISBN 13: 978-0-8048-3845-0
            ISBN 10: 0-8048-3845-3
Printed in Malaysia

Distributed by
North America, Latin America and Europe
Tuttle Publishing, 364 Innovation Drive
North Clarendon, VT 05759-9436 U.S.A.
Tel: 1 (802) 773-8930 Fax: 1 (802) 773-6993
info@tuttlepublishing.com
www.tuttlepublishing.com

Japan
Tuttle Publishing, Yaekari Building,
3rd Floor, 5-4-12 Osaki,
Shinagawa-ku, Tokyo 141 0032
Tel: (81) 3 5437-0171; Fax: (81) 3 5437-0755
tuttle-sales@gol.com

Asia Pacific
Berkeley Books Pte Ltd. 130 Joo Seng Road #06-01
Singapore 368357
Tel: (65) 6280-1330 Fax: (65) 6280-6290
inquiries@periplus.com.sg
www.periplus.com

10 09 08 07   5 4 3 2

TUTTLE PUBLISHING® is a registered trademark of Tuttle Publishing,
a division of Periplus Editions (HK) Ltd.

Contents

A Communal Affair

Fondue has always been a communal affair. In the old days, people ate from one pot in the center of the table, without the niceties of plates and forks. The Swiss elevated fondue to an art form, and its origin rests squarely in the Alps, particularly in the canton of Neuchâtel or Neuenburg. Today, fondue is a popular Swiss restaurant dish, particularly in ski areas. Waiters speedily bring bubbling fondue pots, known as *caquelons*, resting them on high standing trivets over a small alcohol flame. Chefs compete to produce the best fondue in the canton. And diners revel in affixing small bits of bread or other morsels onto the tips of long forks and immersing them into the tabletop cauldrons. Cuisine à la minute never had a more precise meaning.

The word fondue is French for "melted." And traditional Swiss fondue is made of a blend of cheeses melted with wine, beer or liqueur. But today, vegetables, fruits, meat, and seafood are also popular. The Swiss divide fondue into five categories: cheese, Burgundian (oil), Bacchus (wine), Asian and chocolate. For Burgundian fondue, raw meats and other foods are cooked at the table in a pot of rapidly simmering oil, then served with an array of dipping sauces. Bacchus fondue, named after the ancient god of wine, substitutes wine or beer as the cooking medium, while chocolate fondue is a favorite for desserts. Asian fondues begin with either boiling water or broth, usually served in a distinct doughnut-shaped firepot. Meat and vegetables are cooked at the table in the liquid, and the enriched broth is then served as a finale. This dish is variously known as hot pot, firepot or steamboat.

Fondue, of course, is more than liquid or sauce in a fondue pot. It is also the raw and blanched vegetables or cubed breads, meats, and fruits that are cooked or dipped in the fondue. Dipping sauces and often salad are served alongside. For example, a cheese fondue may be accompanied by pickled onions, boiled potatoes, and cucumbers, while Burgundian and Bacchus fondues are served with béarnaise sauce, mayonnaise, and condiments such as mustard, ketchup (tomato sauce), and chutney. Both fresh and dried fruits ideally accompany chocolate fondues, along with cookies such as macaroons, ladyfingers, and cubes of cake.

Whether fondue is Western or Asian in concept, sweet or savory, four to six people is the optimum number at a fondue dinner. More guests than that results in too many people reaching too far across the table into too small a pot. Each diner should be equipped with his or her own plate or bowl and, ideally, individual bowls of dipping sauce, allowing guests to "double dip" with impunity.

Step-by-step Guide

Cheese Fondue

With cheese fondue, cubes of bread and sometimes pieces of boiled potato, vegetables, and cooked meats are dipped in a luscious melted cheese sauce. Ideally, a classic cheese fondue requires well-aged imported Swiss cheeses such as Emmentaler or Gruyère. Most New World Swiss-style cheeses, however, are not sufficiently matured to make a classic fondue. Just as Cheddar is commonly available as mild, sharp, and extra sharp in English-speaking countries, Gruyère and Emmentaler come in varying degrees of pungency when sold in the Alps. The subtle blending of these different cheese flavors is a distinguishing characteristic of the authentic cheese fondues served in Switzerland.

In England, America, and other English-speaking countries, a wide assortment of cheeses can be used in melted-cheese dishes. England and colonial America both produced versions of rarebit, or rabbit, sometimes substituting strong ale or stout for Continental wines. Feta and other fresh sheep's-and goat's-milk cheeses, including blue-veined varieties, melt sufficiently when bound with either flour or cornstarch (cornflour). To make the nacho-like fondue spiked with chopped green chilies, Monterey Jack may be used as a substitute for the Mexican cheeses of Asadero or Queso Chihuahua. Mozzarella is also a suitable substitute.

The most common Swiss cheeses for fondue are Emmentaler and Gruyère. Although varying in flavor, other cheeses that melt particularly well are aged English Lancashire and Cheshire cheeses; Italian Fontina, Provolone, and Mozzarella; and American Jack cheese. Although a common addition to melting blends, and an essential ingredient in rarebit, Cheddar curdles easily and becomes grainy. Many blue-veined cheeses melt reasonably well.

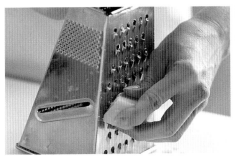

1 Dice or coarsely shred the cheese.

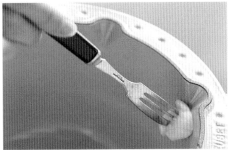

2 Rub the inside of a saucepan or fondue pot with a garlic clove. The garlic remnants may either be finely chopped and added to the pot, or discarded.

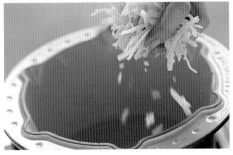

3 Heat the liquid, in this case wine and lemon juice, in a saucepan or as here, in a fondue pot. When the liquid is hot, reduce the heat to low and add the grated cheese.

4 Stir the mixture using figure-8 movements to melt the cheese. Do not melt too quickly over too high a heat, or the cheese will become tough and stringy. Instead, heat it very gradually.

5 Dissolve the potato flour or cornstarch (cornflour) in kirsch, vodka, or a similar distilled spirit. Stir this mixture into the fondue to bind and stabilize it, as well as to add flavor. Cook for a minute or two longer, adding freshly ground white pepper and freshly grated nutmeg or other spices.

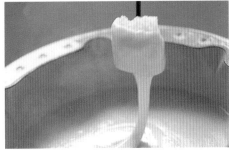

6 If the fondue has been prepared in a saucepan, warm a fondue pot and pour the mixture into it. Serve at the table, over a raised trivet and alcohol flame. (**Note:** a candle flame is insufficient.) Spear bread cubes onto long-handled fondue forks and dip them into the cheese, swirling to coat neatly and to prevent dripping. Eat directly from the fork.

Bacchus Fondue (Wine Fondue)

Dry white acidic wines are most suited to cheese fondue, because the acid helps to prevent lumps. You may also add 1 teaspoon of lemon juice per $^1/_3$ cup (90 ml) wine to reinforce this tartness. Old-world wines, such as very dry Riesling or Italian Frascati, are also suitable, but floral New World wines rich in fruit, such as Chenin Blanc, oaky Chardonnay, and some Sauvignon Blancs, are less ideal. Similarly, a dry (hard) cider wine may be used, but most New World cider tends to be sweet and fruity. Red wine is not traditionally used in fondues.

Spirits used in Bacchus fondues are more variable, although generally dry by tradition. Sherry, Asian rice wines, even beer, ale, and stout may be used. The only restriction is alcohol content. Spirits may catch fire when heated, so they should not be used. Kirsch, a clear cherry liqueur, is the most common liquor used in cheese fondue. Besides adding flavor, kirsch is also drunk during the meal, when it is called *le coup du milieu*, or "the mid-meal shot." Kirsch aficionados are wont to dip their bread into kirsch before the fondue pot.

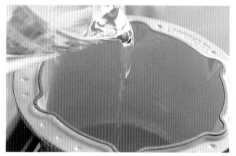 

1 Pour just enough dry white wine into a fondue pot to fill it by about $^2/_3$; heat to a rapid simmer. If desired, add 1 or 2 bouillon cubes for added flavor.

2 Thread a piece of vegetable or a meat strip on a skewer, plunge it into the simmering wine, and cook. Remove cooked food from the liquid, drain, then dip into an assortment of accompanying dipping sauces.

Note: Because of wine's acidity, fondue pots made of stoneware or nonreactive metals should be used for Bacchus Fondues. Don't use aluminum, and if using copper, make sure that it is well lined with tin, nickel, or stainless steel. Exposed patches of copper are toxic.

Burgundian Fondue (Oil Fondue)

Burgundian fondue is actually Swiss in origin. The reason it's called Burgundian is peculiar. Although there appears to be no clear link between Burgundy and oil-bathed food cooked at the table, one anecdote is that a Swiss restaurateur had a restaurant in that part of France, and later, when he relocated to Switzerland, coined the term "fondue bourguignonne."

With Burgundian fondue, a metal pot (either stainless steel or cast iron) should be used. Pieces of raw meat are cooked in simmering oil, then dipped in an assortment of dipping sauces. Since the meat cooks quickly, tender cuts should be used: beef tenderloin; boneless, skinless chicken breast; pork and lamb tenderloin. Skewers are preferred to forks, as they allow diners to pierce through the meat, so the skewers protrude $1/2$ in (12 mm) at the other end and can rest on the bottom of the pot, which keeps the meat from sticking to the pot. Use a good oil such as grapeseed or peanut, as these withstand high temperatures without smoking. Clarified butter also withstands frying temperatures without burning (page 24).

1 Fill a metal fondue pot no more than $1/3$ full with oil, preferably grapeseed or peanut oil. At the table, heat oil to 325–350 °F (165–175 °C), or until simmering. Once the oil is hot, do not move the pot.

2 Spear a piece of vegetable or meat with a skewer, pushing the skewer through so that it protrudes by $1/2$ in (12 mm) at the other end. Skewer then rests on pan bottom, preventing food from touching the pot and sticking.

Cautions when cooking with oil, butter, or ghee

- Do NOT use the traditional cheese fondue pot made of stoneware for Burgundian or oil fondue, as the high heat of simmering oil can crack this material. A cast iron or stainless steel pot is essential for Burgundian fondue.
- Be vigilant when cooking with oil at the table. When moist food comes in contact with hot oil, it literally explodes with vapor. For this reason, cook only a few pieces at a time. For tabletop cooking, use a lower temperature than on a stove top. The oil should be gently simmering, not boiling.
- Never fill the fondue pot more than $1/3$ full of oil, butter, or ghee, and never leave the pot unattended, or shift or move a pot of hot oil.
- In case of a fire, do not douse with water. This can spread the flame. Use a fire blanket or fire extinguisher.

Chocolate Fondue

For chocolate fondue, always use the best chocolate available. Chocolate is commonly divided into two types: pure and compound. Couverture, which is the highest grade of pure chocolate, is also known as dipping chocolate and is made from cocoa liqueur and cocoa butter. The more cocoa it contains, the darker (and more expensive) it is. (Semisweet and bittersweet chocolates fall under this category, but unsweetened chocolate is not suited for these recipes). By contrast, compound (or less-expensive) chocolate, which includes most chocolate chips, is made of cocoa powder plus flavorings and stable vegetable fats. As its name implies, milk chocolate is dark chocolate diluted with milk. Because of this dilution, it is slightly cheaper. White chocolate is not really chocolate at all, although it is made from cocoa butter plus milk, sugar, vanilla and lecithin.

Always use a good grade of chocolate, preferably couverture, and melt it over low heat, to prevent burning. Steam and droplets of water must be avoided when melting chocolate, or it will seize into a stiff mass. Melt milk chocolate at a lower temperature than pure chocolate. To melt chocolate in a microwave, cook chocolate, uncovered, at 70 per cent power for 1 minute at a time, or until it looks half melted; stir until smooth.

1 Finely chop the chocolate into small pieces, about $1/4$ in (6 mm) in diameter. This allows the chocolate to melt evenly.

2 Combine the liquids (here, cream and liqueur) in a double boiler or a bowl placed in a saucepan over barely simmering water. Add the chocolate all at once and stir until it is melted and combined with the liquid. (**Note**: Never attempt to melt the chocolate before the liquid, as it may seize. Because chocolate burns easily, it should not be melted over a direct flame. Melt milk chocolate at an even lower temperature.

3 Cut the other ingredients into bite-sized pieces. Peel, pit, or stem fresh fruit as necessary shortly before serving. Drain and pat dry canned fruits before arranging on a platter. To avoid discoloration, sprinkle with lemon juice.

4 Set a fondue pot over a candle flame or Bunsen burner to warm, but do not overheat or the chocolate will be scorched when it is added. Alternatively, rinse a fondue pot in hot water, dry carefully with a kitchen cloth, and keep in a warm spot until needed. (**Note**: the pot must be absolutely dry before adding the chocolate or the chocolate will seize.) Then pour the chocolate into the warmed fondue pot. Spear a piece of fruit with a fondue fork and dip it into the melted chocolate. Cookies are best handled with the fingers.

Asian Fondue (Firepot or Steamboat)

Like Western fondue, the Asian hot pot began in an era when wood-burning and charcoal stoves were used for heating. To conserve precious fuel, a pot of broth was set atop a brazier, and small pieces of food were cooked in the vessel.

Asian fondues go by many names: *huoguo*, *shabu shabu*, *lau*, and *sin sul lo*. In the West, they are variously called Mongolian hot pots, firepots and steamboats. As in a Bacchus fondue, foods are cooked in a poaching liquid. Asian fondues, however, are traditionally cooked in a large, doughnut-shaped pot. The larger circumference of the pot allows for the simultaneous cooking of more foods than a smaller pot. Chopsticks and small wire-mesh baskets are used to remove the foods from the simmering broth, and they are then dipped into a sauce. The broth becomes richer with the addition of each round of meat and vegetable, and after all the pieces of food have been cooked, cooked rice or noodles are added to the broth, then ladled out into small soup bowls as a delicious finale.

The steaming liquid is the source for the name steamboat, while firepot takes its name from the smoking center chimney filled with hot coals. The pots are commonly made of brass and stainless steel, but inexpensive aluminum versions may be found on the market; electric models are also available. In all cases, it is essential to add the liquid before heating the pot; otherwise, the solder joins of the pot might melt from the heat of the coals. When using steamboats on the table, be sure to place a heatproof trivet or brick beneath it on a tabletop. When burning charcoal indoors, make sure that the room is very well ventilated. Charcoal releases carbon monoxide, so if anyone at the table begins to feel drowsy, open the windows immediately.

Alternatives to hot pots include a metal fondue pot, or for more authenticity, a large pottery sand pot, chrysanthemum bowl, or Japanese *donabe*, set atop a raised trivet with an alcohol flame underneath. A wok sitting on a portable gas base also works well, but carbon steel woks tend to rust over long exposure to liquid; so a nonstick or stainless steel wok is preferable.

1 Light a small pile of lump or natural charcoal in a fireplace or in an outdoor grill. Natural charcoal is preferable to charcoal briquettes because it's pure and burns at a higher temperature. Mound the charcoal around an electric fire starter, plug it in, and after 7 minutes remove the starter. Alternatively, light charcoal in a charcoal chimney: tightly wad newspaper in its base, place charcoal on top, and set the newspaper alight. Do not use instant lighter fluids, firesticks, or other chemical fire agents, as these may produce unpleasant fumes at the table. Never use gasoline or kerosene, as both are dangerously explosive. Pour hot broth into the firepot or metal fondue pot to fill it about $2/_3$ full.

2 Once the coals are covered with a layer of white ash, after about 20 minutes, use long-handled metal tongs to transfer them into the chimney of the pot. Wear a heavy oven mitt in case some charcoal falls and requires quick retrieval. Add hot coals to the center of the chimney pot, filling it no more than halfway. Bring the broth to a rapid simmer. (**Note**: if the pot has a lid attached to the chimney stack, remove it during cooking; cover to douse the flame. Conversely, many models have a ring lid for the stock; this should be in place to sufficiently raise the broth temperature prior to cooking.)

3 Use small wire-mesh baskets, chopsticks, and tongs to dip raw foods into the broth and retrieve the cooked ingredients from the pot, and then use chopsticks to dip them into the accompanying sauces. (**Note**: Wire-mesh baskets come in a variety of sizes and are available in Asian markets and cookware stores, as are chopsticks and tongs. After guests have finished eating the meat and vegetables, add cooked rice or soaked noodles to the broth. Heat through and ladle into soup bowls. However, some broths, such as Vietnamese *lau*, are too pungent to eat as soup.)

Essential Fondue Ingredients

Ale: Traditionally, ale was made without hops, and therefore lacked the slight bitterness of beer. Today, there is little difference between ale and other beers. Substitute lager.

Appenzeller: One of the three most common Swiss cheeses, Appenzeller's aroma is slightly spicy, with hints of fermenting fruit. Although it may have a few large holes, they will not be as prevalent as in Emmentaler.

Beaufort: Regarded as the finest of the French Gruyère cheese family. See Gruyère and Emmentaler.

Blue: An internal mold cheese with green-blue col-

ored veining. The classic blue is French Roquefort, made from sheep's milk. Other blues are commonly made from cow's milk, and more rarely goat's milk. Although varying in taste and texture, blue cheeses are largely interchangeable in most recipes. Other notable blues include Gorgonzola from Italy, which sometimes comes blended with mascarpone; Bleu de Bresse; Fourme d'Ambert; English stilton; and a plethora of crumbly cow's-milk blues.

Cantal: This firm cheese could loosely be called the French version of Cheddar, although it has a delicately sour under-taste. Use interchangeably with mild to medium Cheddar.

Cellophane noodles: Commonly known as bean threads or glass noodles, these very thin strands are generally made from mung beans. Soak in hot to boiling

water until translucent before using. Cellophane noodles can easily be distinguished from rice noodles by their pliable elasticity. Brittle rice noodles break easily, while bean noodles do not.

Cheshire: A traditional English cow's-milk cheese. Like Cheddar, this was originally a cloth-wrapped cartwheel, but is now more commonly sold in rectangular bricks.

Clarified butter: An unsalted butter that has the milk solids and water removed from the butter, so all that remains is pure liquid golden-yellow butter fat. It is a preferred type of butter for sautéing because it has a higher smoke point, and it also has a longer shelf-life. If you prefer to make your own, clarified butter can be easily prepared using normal butter (page 24). Ghee is a type of clarified butter used extensively in Indian cuisine.

Coconut milk/cream: Canned unsweetened coconut milk and cream is available at all Asian grocers and most supermarkets. Do not use sweetened "cream of coconut," which is specially created for desserts or alcohol drinks like piña coladas. When purchasing coconut milk and cream, note that "cream" is the thickest, "milk" is thinner, and "water" refers to the watery juice in the center of a coconut shell. When a label fails to clearly identify the product, shake the can. The thicker it is, the less it will splash. Once home, place the can in the refrigerator and the richest portion will rise to the top; carefully spoon it off.

Colby: A washed-curd cow's-milk cheese, colby cheese originated in America but is now made world-wide. The cheese is soft and slightly elastic, and innocuously mild.

Comté: A member of the French Gruyère cheese family, Comté has pea-sized holes. See also Gruyère and Emmentaler.

Edam: Easily identifiable because of its red ball shape, Edam is usually sold young, and its texture is creamy and flavor mild. Aged Edam, although rare, has a good flavor when melted.

Emmentaler: The famous cheese of Switzerland with holes in it, Emmentaler is commonly confused with the hole-less Gruyère. Although similar, it's aroma is sweeter, and its texture smoother and more elastic. French-made Emmental is similar.

Feta: The best and creamiest Feta Cheeses are made from sheep's and goat's milk; cow's-milk Feta is much firmer. Feta is brined and consequently is very salty, with a distinct tang.

Fish sauce: A salty, pungent Southeast Asian seasoning made from fermented fish. It is especially popular in Thailand and Vietnam, where it is known as *nam pla* and *nuoc mam*, respectively.

Fontina: A mild and creamy cheese from Italy, Fontina becomes soft at room temperature. It has the sweetness of Emmentaler and the tang of Gruyère, and a suggestion of Port-Salut.

Substitute with a young version of any of those cheeses, a Tilsit, or preferably, a Fribourg Vacherin.

Galangal: A rhizome related (and similar) to fresh ginger, galangal is especially popular in Thai dishes.

Gorgonzola: See Blue.

Gouda: A Dutch cow's-milk cheese resembling a strong-tasting Edam. When young, this is a mild-tasting cheese, creamy in texture, faintly sweet and fruity. Mature Gouda, which is aged for several years, becomes very hard and easy to grate.

Gruyère: A firm to hard cow's-cheese from Switzerland, nutty yet earthy in character. Confusingly, "Gruyère" is also generically used to describe similar

French mountain cheeses such as Comté, Beaufort, and Emmental. Unlike Emmentaler and Swiss-style variants, Gruyère has no holes.

Hard cider: Fermented apple juice, not to be confused with nonalcoholic apple cider. European apple cider commonly tastes bone dry, with little or no residual sugar or fresh fruit flavor. This is the preferred style to use in fondue.

Monterey Jack: A very mild white cheese made from cow's milk. Popular in the United States, this cheese is used in Southwestern Tex-Mex dishes and Cal-Mex dishes. Substitute colby, mozzarella, or Münster.

Jarslberg: See Swiss-style cheese.

Kimchi: A Korean pickle, usually cabbage but also diakon radish and cucumber, fermented and fiery with chili.

Kirsch: A clear cherry distillate, or Eau-de-Vie.

Konbu: A variety of dried kelp from Japan, and an essential ingredient in the Japanese soup stock known as *dashi*. It is available in Japanese grocery stores and at select health food outlets.

Lancashire: English cow's-cheese, crumbly and mild, but sharper with age. Use as a substitute for Cheddar in Welsh rarebit.

Mascarpone: A cultured-cream, with a sweet yet slightly acidic taste. It is traditionally made from the cream skimmed during the manufacture of Parmesan cheese.

Parmesan: A hard, strong-tasting cheese used as a topping and a flavoring.

Pizza cheese: Grated cheese sold generically in supermarkets, usually a blend of one or more cheeses, such as Mozzarella, Colby, mild Cheddar, Jack, and sometimes Parmesan. Depending on the blend—especially when there is a dominant Cheddar or Parmesan content—this cheese may prove unreliable in a fondue.

Porter: Traditionally a blend of pale beer, brown beer and stale ale, porter is similar to stout, but not so strong. If unavailable, use stout.

Port-Salut: A semi-soft cow's-cheese with a bright orange rind. Slightly nutty, it is milder in taste than it looks. Originally, it was made by monks in France. Substitute a Chaumes or St Paulin.

Provolone: Commonly sold in large, white-waxed balls or huge cylinders, tied with a cord and hanging from a rack. This cow's-milk cheese, originally from Italy, is now widely manufactured overseas. Young Provolone is mild and supple, while aged Provolone has a strong, pungent flavor.

Raclette: Versions of this cow's-milk cheese, originally from the Valais, are today made abroad. Their taste is usually less well aged and distinctive when compared to that of their Swiss counterparts. Raclette cheese has a creamy consistency that melts easily but does not run. Semi-firm cheeses such as Tilsit and German-style Münster may be substituted. Raclette is also served as a table cheese.

Rice paper: Thin and brittle spring roll wrappers made from rice starch. These require soaking before use. Round rice paper are known in Vietnamese as *bénh tráng*, and are available from Asian grocery stores.

Rice vinegar: A mild vinegar, especially popular in east Asia. Rice vinegar does not have as strong an acidity as Western vinegar. Do not substitute with seasoned rice vinegar, or with Chinese black vinegar, which is usually made from wheat, millet, and sorghum.

Rice wine: Chinese cooking wine is brewed from glutinous rice and millet. Japanese sake, although more expensive, may be substituted, as may dry sherry. Chinese Shaoxing wine, although made from rice, may prove too dominant in flavor, as it is well aged. Do not substitute sweetened rice wines, such as Japanese mirin.

Sapsago (Schabzieger): A hard, green-imbued cone-shaped cheese, assertive in flavor. Freshly grated Parmesan has a similar texture—but not flavor—to Sapsago, and may be substituted.

Shaoxing wine: See Rice wine.

Soy sauce: Chinese light soy sauce is similar to standard Japanese soy sauce. Do not use Chinese dark or sweet soy sauce. All Japanese soy sauces in the international market are naturally brewed, not chemically manufactured.

Stout: A very dark to black beer, renowned for its creamy head. Its faintly sweet taste is countered with the bitterness of hops. The most famous brand of stout is Guinness.

Swiss-style cheese: A generic cheese only faintly resembling Emmentaler, with large holes. Generally it has little pronounced flavor, and it is available in small rectangles. A better substitute is Norwegian Jarslberg.

Tilsit: A firm cow's-milk cheese of both Dutch and German heritage. It is faintly piquant and similar in taste to Gouda, although the primary difference is its washed rind that forms into a hard crust.

Tomme or **tome**: A generic term for cheese, commonly (but not exclusively) the hard mountain styles such as Beaufort. The celebrated Tomme de Savoie is made from cow's milk, while a distant Pyrenees version may be sheep's milk. Both cheeses can be used in fondues.

Vacherin: Fribourg Vacherin, or Vacherin Fribourgeois, is a creamier version of Gruyère, yet its flavor is less savory. Substitute French Reblochon. The similarly named "Vacherin Mont d'Or" is not interchangeable.

Sauces and Dips

Mounted Béarnaise Sauce

4 tablespoons (60 ml) dry white
   wine
3 eggs, separated
3 tablespoons tarragon vinegar
2 Asian shallots, very finely
   chopped
2 teaspoons chopped fresh
   tarragon, or 1 teaspoon dried
   tarragon
$1/_2$ teaspoon coarsely-ground
   white pepper
$1/_2$ teaspoon salt
$3/_4$ cup (185 ml) Clarified Butter
   (page 24), melted and cooled to
   room temperature
1 tablespoon chopped fresh parsley
1 teaspoon chopped fresh chervil
   (optional)

1 In a small bowl, beat 2 tablespoons of wine into the egg yolks and set aside. In a large bowl, beat the egg whites until stiff, glossy peaks form and set aside.
2 In a small saucepan, combine the remaining 2 table-spoons of wine, the vinegar, shallots, tarragon, and pepper. Boil the mixture until reduced to a glaze, about 5 minutes. Remove from the heat and allow to cool.
3 Whisk in the egg yolks and salt. Set the saucepan in a skillet of barely simmering water. Whisk constantly until the mixture is thick and creamy. Remove from the heat and very gradually whisk in the melted butter, returning the pan to the simmering water periodically to keep the sauce warm. Gently fold in the beaten egg whites, parsley, and if using, chervil. Serve warm.

Makes 2 cups (500 ml)

Anchovy Sauce

One 2-oz (60-g) can anchovy
   fillets, drained
4 tablespoons milk
4 tablespoons (60 g) butter
$1/_2$ cup (125 ml) olive oil
2 cloves garlic, very finely chopped
$1/_4$ teaspoon coarsely-ground
   white pepper
$1/_2$ cup (20 g) chopped fresh
   parsley
Salt, to taste

1 In a small bowl, soak the anchovy fillets in the milk for about 15 minutes, then drain and discard the milk. Finely chop the anchovy fillets.
2 In a small saucepan, melt the butter with the oil over medium heat. Reduce the heat to medium low, add the garlic and sauté until fragrant, about 2 minutes.
3 Add the chopped anchovy and pepper, and cook for about 15 minutes. Stir in the parsley and salt. Serve warm.

Makes $3/_4$ cup (185 ml)

Curried Mayonnaise

2 eggs at room temperature
1 tablespoon freshly-squeezed
   lemon juice
1 teaspoon salt
$1/_4$ teaspoon finely-ground white
   pepper
1 cup (250 ml) peanut oil
$1/_2$ cup (125 ml) olive oil
1 tablespoon ground red pepper
1 teaspoon dijon mustard

Makes $1^1/_2$ cups (375 ml)

In a food processor, combine 1 whole egg and 1 egg yolk (reserve the remaining egg white for another use), the lemon juice, salt and pepper, and process for 5 seconds. With the machine running, very gradually drizzle in the oil in a very thin stream to make a thick sauce. Add the ground red pepper and mustard, and process until very thick.

Note: If the mayonnaise separates, pour the mixture into a small jug. Thoroughly wash the blender or food processor container. Add 1 whole egg and process for a few seconds. With the machine running, very gradually add the separated mixture. The mayonnaise should rebind.

Variation: A quick version may be made by stirring 1 tablespoon of ground red pepper into 1 cup (250 ml) of commercial mayonnaise.

Drawn Butter

$1/_2$ cup (125 g) butter, preferably
   salted, cut into small cubes and
   chilled
3 tablespoons flour
2 cups (500 ml) boiling water
$1/_4$ teaspoon coarsely ground
   white pepper
1 tablespoon freshly-squeezed
   lemon juice
$1/_2$ teaspoon salt, or to taste

Melt $1/_2$ of the butter in a saucepan over medium heat. Whisk in the flour and cook for 2 to 3 minutes. Gradually whisk in the boiling water, and cook until smooth, then add the pepper and lemon juice. Reduce the heat to low and simmer for 5 minutes. Whisk in the remaining butter, piece by piece, until incorporated. Add the salt and remove from the heat. Serve warm.

Makes 2 cups

Quick Ponzu Sauce

1/2 cup (125 ml) soy sauce
2 1/2 tablespoons freshly-squeezed
  lemon juice

In a small bowl, combine all the ingredients. Pour the sauce into individual dipping bowls. Serve the same day it is made.

Makes 2/3 cup (150 ml)

Nuoc Cham Dipping Sauce

2 small cloves garlic
2 small finger-length red chili peppers, deseeded and chopped
1 1/2 tablespoons sugar
Juice of 1 lime
4 tablespoons fish sauce
1/2 cup (125 ml) water

In a mortar, grind the garlic and chili together with a pestle to make a paste. Add all the other ingredients and stir until dissolved.

Makes 1 cup (250 ml)

Quick Chinese Mustard

1/4 cup (20 g) mustard powder
2 tablespoons warm water
Soy sauce, to taste (optional)

Makes 1/3 cup (90 ml)

Place the mustard in a small bowl and gradually blend in just enough water to make a smooth paste. Let stand for 10 minutes before serving. If desired, thin with a little soy sauce. This is a very piquant sauce, and a little goes a long way.

Aromatic Oil Marinade

2 Asian shallots, very finely
  chopped
2 cloves garlic, very finely
  chopped
$1/2$ in (12 mm) fresh ginger root,
  finely grated
Grated rind of 1 orange
Grated rind of 1 lime or lemon
Few sprigs of fresh thyme,
  or 1 teaspoon dried thyme
2 teaspoons coarsely-ground
  white pepper
1 teaspoon salt (optional)
$1/2$ cup (125 ml) olive oil

Combine all the ingredients in a shallow casserole dish
and mix well.

Makes $2/3$ cup (150 ml)

Mongolian Firepot Dip

$3/4$ cup (185 ml) soy sauce
4 tablespoons peanut oil
1 tablespoon grated fresh ginger
1 green onion, finely chopped
2 tablespoons coarsely-chopped
  fresh cilantro (coriander leaves)
Pinch of cayenne pepper (optional)

In a small saucepan, bring the soy sauce and oil to a
boil over high heat. Immediately remove from the heat
and add the ginger and onion. Set aside to cool and
pour the dip into individual sauce dishes. Just before
serving, add the cilantro and cayenne, if using.

Makes 1 cup (250 ml)

Mizutaki Sauce

2 eggs
4 tablespoons rice vinegar
$^1/_2$ teaspoon mustard powder
$^1/_3$ cup (90 ml) good-quality
   oil such as grapeseed or
   cold-pressed vegetable
Pinch of salt

In a blender, combine all the ingredients and process until frothy, about 5 seconds. Spoon the sauce into individual dipping bowls.

Makes 1 cup (250 ml)

Korean Vinegar Dipping Sauce

3 tablespoons sesame seeds,
   toasted (page 69)
$^1/_2$ cup (125 ml) soy sauce
2 tablespoons rice vinegar
$^1/_2$ in (12 mm) fresh ginger root,
   grated
Pinch of sugar
Pinch of cayenne pepper
$^1/_2$ green onion, minced

In a mortar, lightly grind the sesame seeds with a pestle. Stir in all the other ingredients except the green onion. Immediately before serving, stir in the green onion and serve in individual dipping bowls.

Makes $^3/_4$ cup (185 ml)

Clarified Butter

2 lbs (1 kg) unsalted butter

Makes 3 cups (750 ml)

1 Melt the butter in a double boiler over simmering water. Remove from the heat and set aside so the milk solids will settle to the bottom. Skim off any foam.
2 Carefully pour or ladle the clear yellow liquid through a sieve lined with cheesecloth (muslin), making sure to leave all the white solids in the pan. Store in a sealed jar in the refrigerator.

Chicken Broth

1 chicken (3 lbs/1$^1/_2$ kg), whole
  or cut up
12 cups (3 liters) water
$^1/_2$ in (12 mm) fresh ginger root,
  thinly sliced
2 green onions, white part only,
  washed well and chopped
1 tablespoon soy sauce

Makes 8–10 cups (2–2$^1/_2$ liters)

1 Rinse the chicken well under cold running water. Place it in a narrow, tall stockpot and add the water to cover the chicken. Bring to a boil over medium heat, uncovered. Skim to remove the foam.
2 Add all the other ingredients, reduce the heat to low and simmer for about 1$^1/_2$ hours. Remove from the heat, strain and set aside to cool.
3 Cover the clear broth and refrigerate overnight. Remove and discard the congealed fat.

Enriched Meat Stock

1 pig's foot (2 lbs/1 kg)
1 lb (500 g) pork shoulder, sliced
  into cubes
12 cups (3 liters) water
1 carrot, peeled and chopped
1 bunch celery leaves, roughly
  chopped
1 bay leaf
$^1/_2$ teaspoon peppercorns
Salt, to taste

Makes 8–10 cups (2–2$^1/_2$ liters)

1 Blanch the pig's foot in boiling water for 1 minute. Drain and place it in the stockpot with the pork shoulder. Add the water to cover the pork. Bring to a boil over medium heat, uncovered. Skim to remove the foam.
2 Add all the other ingredients, reduce the heat to low and simmer for about 1$^1/_2$ hours. Remove from the heat, strain and set aside to cool.
3 Cover the clear broth and refrigerate overnight. Remove and discard the congealed fat.

Note: For Asian dishes, leave out the vegetables and peppercorns.

Classic Cheese Fondue

1 clove garlic
1 cup (250 ml) dry white wine
10 oz (300 g) Emmentaler cheese,
  diced or shredded
10 oz (300 g) Gruyère cheese,
  diced or shredded
$1^1/_2$ tablespoons potato flour or
  cornstarch (cornflour), mixed
  with 4 tablespoons kirsch liqueur
$^1/_4$ teaspoon ground white pepper
Pinch of freshly grated nutmeg
Crusty bread, cut into cubes,
  to serve

Note: If the fondue is too thin, add more cheese. If too thick, add more wine.

Suggested quantities
Bread: 1 loaf per 2–3 persons, or about twenty 1-in ($2^1/_2$-cm) cubes per person

Serves 4–6

1 Rub a medium, heavy saucepan with the garlic cloves. Discard the garlic. Pour the wine into the saucepan and bring just to a boil over medium-high heat. Reduce the heat to low and add the cheese, stirring slowly in a figure-8 pattern until the cheese has just melted. It should melt very slowly—about 5 minutes in all—or it may become stringy and tough. Add the potato flour or cornstarch mixture, pepper, and nutmeg and simmer for 2 more minutes. The fondue should gently sputter, not boil. (The fondue should be thick enough to just cover the bread; it will thicken at the table.)
2 Pour the fondue into a warmed fondue pot and serve immediately. At the table, guests should take several cubes of bread onto their plates, skewer one with a fork and dip it into the pot, then eat directly from the fork.

Fondue variations
The mildest-tasting fondue is made solely of Emmentaler cheese. For a medium-flavored fondue, combine $^1/_2$ Emmentaler and $^1/_2$ Gruyère. Stronger yet is the blending of $^1/_3$ Emmentaler and $^2/_3$ Gruyère, while the most pungent fondue is made from only well-matured Gruyère. The following are other famed Swiss variations.
Jura: Mince 2 green onions and sauté in 1 tablespoon of butter. Add the wine and proceed as in the above recipe.
Vaud: Finely chop 2 cloves garlic and add to the wine, then proceed as in the above recipe.
Appenzell: Substitute hard cider for the wine, and use equal amounts of grated Appenzeller and Fribourg vacherin instead of Emmentaler and Gruyère.
Fribourg: Use only Fribourg vacherin and melt it in $^1/_3$ cup (90 ml) of hot water. Omit the wine and cornstarch. Serve with chats boiled in their jackets instead. (This fondue burns easily, so be sure to use very low heat.)
Glarus: Omit the wine. Melt 4 tablespoons (60 g) of butter in a saucepan and add 2 tablespoons of flour. Stir over low heat for 2 minutes, taking care not to brown. Add 10 oz (300 g) each shredded Gruyère and Sapsago (Schabzieger cheese), stirring until melted. Proceed as in the master recipe.

Fresh Green Herbs Fondue

1 small clove garlic
1 cup (250 ml) medium-dry
  white wine
1 tablespoon freshly-squeezed
  lemon juice
1$^1/_4$ lbs (625 g) Edam or Gouda
  cheese, shredded
1 tablespoon potato flour or
  cornstarch (cornflour)
4 tablespoons chopped
  fresh parsley
2 tablespoons chopped fresh chives
2 teaspoons dried tarragon
Pinch of cayenne pepper
$^1/_2$ teaspoon ground white pepper
1 tablespoon gin
Slices of crusty bread,
  raw vegetables and cooked
  meats of choice, to serve

1 Rub a medium, heavy saucepan with the garlic clove. Discard the garlic clove. Place the pot over medium-high heat, add the wine and bring just to a boil. Add the lemon juice and reduce the heat to medium-low.
2 Toss the cheese with the potato flour or cornstarch, and add it to the pot by the handful, stirring with each addition until just melted. Then add the herbs, seasonings and gin, and cook for 2 to 3 minutes. Remove from the heat and transfer to a warmed fondue pot. Serve with the bread, vegetables and meats.

Suggested quantities
Meat: 8 oz (250 g) per person
Bread: 1 loaf per 2–3 persons, or about twenty 1-in (2$^1/_2$-cm) cubes per person
Vegetables: 6–8 oz (185–250 g) per person (before trimming)

Serves 4–6

"Pizza" Fondue

2 tablespoons butter

2 ripe tomatoes, peeled, deseeded and chopped

1 large clove garlic, finely chopped

1 small onion, finely chopped

$1/2$ cup (125 ml) dry white wine

2 teaspoons freshly-squeezed lemon juice

1 lb (500 g) shredded Mozzarella cheese

1 tablespoon potato flour or cornstarch (cornflour)

2 tablespoons capers, drained

2 anchovy fillets, coarsely chopped (optional)

$1/2$ teaspoon red chili pepper flakes, or to taste

$1/2$ teaspoon dried oregano

1 teaspoon salt, or to taste

15 black olives, pitted and coarsely chopped

Crusty bread, cut into cubes, to serve

Pepperoni or other dried sausages, cut into $3/4$-in (2-cm) slices, and pineapple chunks, to serve (optional)

1 Melt the butter in a heavy, medium saucepan over medium-high heat. Add the chopped tomato, garlic, and onion. Cook until the onion is translucent, about 3 minutes. Add the wine and lemon juice, and reduce the heat to low. Dust the cheese with the potato flour or cornstarch, and stir it in until melted and smooth, about 5 minutes.

2 Add the capers and anchovy fillets (if using) to the melted cheese, then stir in the red pepper flakes, oregano and salt, and cook for 1 to 2 minutes. Remove the mixture from the heat and transfer to a warmed fondue pot. Top with the chopped olives and serve with the bread cubes, and if desired, sausage and pineapple.

Suggested quantities

Meat: 8 oz (250 g) per person

Bread: 1 loaf per 2–3 persons, or about twenty 1-in ($2^1/_2$-cm) cubes per person

Fruit: 6–8 oz (185–250 g) per person (before peeling and coring)

Fondue variation

For a stronger blend, replace 4 oz (125 g) of the Mozzarella with the same amount of grated Parmesan.

Serves 4–6

Crab and Sharp Cheddar Fondue

$^3/_4$ cup (185 ml) hard cider or beer
1 tablespoon freshly-squeezed
   lemon juice
Pinch of sugar
1 lb (500 g) sharp Cheddar cheese,
   shredded
2 tablespoons flour
7 oz (200 g) fresh lump crabmeat,
   picked over for shells
1 teaspoon caraway seed, lightly
   toasted
$^1/_2$ teaspoon salt, or to taste
Pinch of cayenne pepper
Crusty bread, cut into cubes,
   to serve

1 In a double boiler over simmering water, heat the cider or beer, lemon juice, and sugar over medium-high heat. Meanwhile, toss the cheese with the flour. When the cider or beer mixture is hot, reduce the heat to low, gradually stir in the cheese and let it melt slowly, about 5 minutes.

2 Heat the crabmeat in a microwave on medium high until warm, about 30 seconds. (This helps prevent the cheese from curdling later.) Add the crabmeat, caraway seed, salt and cayenne to the melted cheese. Transfer to a warm fondue pot and serve with the bread cubes.

Suggested quantities
Bread: 1 loaf per 2–3 persons, or about twenty 1-in ($2^1/_2$-cm) cubes per person

Serves 4–6

Fondue Mexicana

1 cup (250 ml) Mexican beer
1 tablespoon freshly-squeezed lemon juice
6 small finger-length chili peppers, deseeded and
  coarsely chopped
$1/2$ bell pepper (capsicum), deseeded and diced
1 lb (500 g) Monterey Jack or mild Mozzarella cheese,
  shredded
2 tablespoons flour
$1/2$ teaspoon paprika
Pinch of ground cumin
1 teaspoon salt, or to taste
Tortilla chips, to serve

1 In a heavy, medium saucepan, heat the beer over
high heat until it foams. Add the lemon juice, chili peppers and bell pepper, and reduce the heat to medium.
2 Toss the cheese with the flour, paprika and cumin,
then add it to the pan, 1 handful at a time, stirring to
melt each handful. Add the salt and transfer to a warm
fondue pot. Serve with the tortilla chips.

Note: Wash your hands, knife and chopping board well
with hot, soapy water after touching the chili peppers,
as their lingering oils will burn the skin.

Serves 4–6

Piedmont Fonduta

1¹/₄ lbs (625 g) cold Italian Fontina cheese, thinly sliced
1 cup (250 ml) milk
1 cup (250 ml) cream (if available, substitute 2 cups
  (500 ml) half-and-half (half cream) for the cream
  and milk)
4 tablespoons butter at room temperature
6 egg yolks, lightly beaten
1 white truffle, thinly sliced or 1–2 tablespoons truffle
  oil (optional)
Slices of crusty bread or cooked rice, to serve (optional)

1 Lay the cheese slices in a 4-cup (1-liter) bowl, over-lapping them slightly. Pour the milk and cream over the cheese. Let stand for at least 2 hours, or overnight. When ready, drain the cream and milk and measure out ¹/₂ cup (125 ml). In a small saucepan, heat the cream and milk over low heat until bubbles form around the edges of the pan. Stir in the butter.
2 Place the cheese in a double boiler over simmering water and stir constantly until melted. Gradually stir in the cream and milk until smooth and creamy, then beat in egg yolks. The mixture should thicken slightly. Immediately transfer to a warmed fondue pot. If using, scatter the truffle slices or drizzle the truffle oil on top.
3 At the table, skewer the bread slices onto forks and dip into the fondue, or spoon the fondue over individual bowls of rice to eat with a table fork. Because of this dish's egg content, it should be maintained over a very low flame and eaten immediately.

Suggested quantities
Bread: 1 loaf per 2–3 persons, or about twenty 1-in (2¹/₂-cm) cubes per person
¹/₂–1 cup (50 g–100 g) cooked rice per person

Serves 4–6

Feta Cheese Melt

4 tablespoons butter
$1/4$ cup (60 ml) olive oil
8 oz (250 g) Feta cheese, crumbled (about $1^1/_2$ cups)
1 cup (250 ml) milk, scalded
2 tablespoons potato flour or cornstarch (cornflour)
    mixed with 2 tablespoons water
One 6-oz (180-g) can crabmeat or shrimp (prawns),
    drained
Pita (pocket) bread, cucumber slices, pickles and
    marinated eggplant, to serve

1 In a small, heavy saucepan, melt the butter with the
oil over medium heat. Add the cheese, stirring until
melted. It will be creamy, but not smooth. Stir in the
milk and cook until the mixture is smooth, then stir in
the flour or cornstarch mixture and cook until thickened,
1 to 2 minutes. Finally stir in the crabmeat or shrimp,
and transfer to a warmed fondue pot.
2 Preheat the broiler (grill). Just before serving, place
the fondue pot under the broiler for about 2 minutes.
Tear the bread into strips, then roll and skewer. Serve
the cucumber, pickles and eggplant alongside.

Note: Sheep's-milk Feta melts more easily than cow's,
but both work well here. If the Feta is too salty, soak it
briefly in fresh water prior to using.

Suggested quantities
Pita bread: 2–3 per person, depending on the size of
the bread
Vegetables: 6–8 oz (185–250 g) per person (before
trimming)

Fondue variation
Substitute dry white wine for the milk.

Serves 4

Blue Cheese Fondue

1/2 cup (125 g) unsalted butter
2 Asian shallots, minced
1 clove garlic, finely chopped
1 cup (250 ml) dry white wine
1 lb (500 g) blue cheese, crumbled
3 egg yolks
1/2 cup (125 ml) Enriched Meat
  Stock (page 25), heated
1/2 teaspoon dried tarragon
1 tablespoon Dijon mustard
1/4 teaspoon salt, or to taste
1/4 teaspoon ground white pepper
Rye bread and/or sourdough
  bread cubes, gherkins or
  cornichons and pickled onions,
  to serve

Serves 4–6

1 In a medium, heavy saucepan, melt the butter over medium-low heat. Sauté the shallots and garlic until translucent, about 3 minutes. Pour in the white wine, increase the heat to medium and cook to reduce to a glaze, about 20 minutes. Remove the pan from the heat and immediately set it over a pot of simmering water. Stir in the cheese until melted.

2 Whisk the egg yolks with the hot stock, then stir briskly into the melted cheese. Add the remaining ingredients and continue cooking until slightly thickened; do not overcook or boil, or it may curdle. Immediately strain into a warm fondue pot and place over very low heat to keep warm. Serve with the bread and pickles.

Suggested quantities
Bread: 1 loaf per 2–3 persons, or about twenty 1-in (2¹/₂-cm) cubes per person

Welsh Rarebit

$^1/_2$ cup (125 g) butter
$^1/_2$ cup (125 ml) beer or ale
1 lb (500 g) extra sharp (extra tasty) Cheddar or Lancashire cheese, shredded
Salt, to taste
$^1/_2$ teaspoon ground white pepper
1–2 loaves toasted bread slices, each cut into 4 triangles, to serve

In a medium saucepan, combine the butter and beer or ale, and heat over medium heat until bubbles appear. Reduce the heat to medium low and add the cheese all at once, stirring until just melted. Add the salt and pepper, then pour the cheese mixture into a warmed fondue pot. Serve with toast.

Note: For a richer rarebit, add 2 tablespoons of bacon fat with a similar amount of butter.

Serves 4–6

Stout Rabbit

$3/4$ cup (185 g) butter
$2/3$ cup (150 ml) stout or porter
1 tablespoon flour
1 lb (500 g) Stilton or blue
  cheese, crumbled
1 tablespoon prepared English
  (hot) mustard
$1/2$ teaspoon ground white pepper
1–2 loaves thin French bread,
  thinly sliced and toasted, to serve

In a medium saucepan, combine the butter and stout or porter and heat over low heat to melt the butter. Whisk in the flour, then gradually add the cheese a little at a time, stirring just until melted. Add the mustard and pepper. Pour the cheese mixture into a warmed fondue pot and serve with the toast, using either fingers or a fork to dip the bread.

Serves 4–6

Raclette

1¹/₄ lbs (625 g) Raclette cheese, in one wedge
1³/₄ lbs (875 g) small new potatoes (chats), boiled in their jackets
Gherkins or cornichons, and pickled onions, to serve

Serves 4

1 Place 4 dinner plates in a very low oven to warm.
2 Place the cheese on a clean cutting board and set before an open fire. When the cheese bubbles and melts, scrape it off with a wide palette knife and spread it onto the warm plates to eat immediately. Repeat as the cheese continues to melt.
3 Use the potatoes to scrape up the cheese and eat with gherkins and onions.

Fondue variation

Preheat the oven to 450°F (230°C). Lay thin slices—about ¹/₈ in (3 mm)—of cheese on individual ramekins or small ovenproof plates that have been lightly brushed with olive oil or butter. Heat in the oven until just melted, about 5 minutes. Serve immediately.

A Fondue of Marinated Meats

3 lbs (1$^1/_2$ kg) beef rib eye steak
  (Scotch fillet), trimmed
Vegetable crudités of choice
4–5 cups (1–1$^1/_4$ liters) dry
  white wine
Mounted Béarnaise Sauce (page 20)
  or other dipping sauces of choice
Crusty bread and green salad,
  to serve

Marinade

3 tablespoons white wine vinegar
4 tablespoons olive or good-quality
  salad or vegetable oil
4 tablespoons dry white wine
1 clove garlic, crushed
1 Asian shallot, finely chopped
1 teaspoon salt
2 teaspoons coarsely-ground
  white pepper

Serves 4–6

1 Slice the beef into thin strips. Combine the Marinade ingredients in a shallow dish and toss with the beef. Cover and refrigerate for at least 2 hours or overnight.
2 Place the vegetables on a platter; cover and refrigerate until ready to use.
3 Prepare the Mounted Béarnaise Sauce following the recipe on page 20. Spoon into individual dipping bowls.
4 Fill a stoneware or metal fondue pot $^2/_3$ full with the wine. At the table, bring the wine just to a rapid simmer. (Alternatively, measure the required amount, heat on the stove, and transfer to the fondue pot.) Drain the marinated beef and place it in a shallow serving dish. Arrange the beef, vegetables, dipping sauce and accompaniments with the pot on the table.
5 To cook the meat and vegetables, thread the meat slices on skewers and spear the vegetables, letting the end of each skewer protrude by $^1/_2$ in (12 mm). Dip the meat in the simmering wine for 2–3 minutes, and the vegetables for 3–5 minutes. Remove from the wine, drain and dip into individual bowls of sauce, and eat with the crusty bread and green salad.

Suggested quantities

Bread: 1 loaf per 2–3 persons, or about twenty 1-in
(2$^1/_2$-cm) cubes per person
Vegetables: 6–8 oz (185–250 g) per person (before trimming)

Fondue variation

Substitute Aromatic Oil Marinade (page 23) for the wine marinade.

La Gitana

La Gitana takes its name from a Spanish sherry.

2 lbs (1 kg) boneless, skinless chicken breasts
1 lb (500 g) veal or pork tenderloin
1 teaspoon salt (optional)
Vegetable crudités of choice
4–5 cups (1–1^1/$_4$ liters) dry sherry
1–2 beef bouillon (stock) cubes (optional)
Mounted Béarnaise Sauce (page 20) and Anchovy
  Sauce (page 20), or other dipping sauces of choice

1 Slice the chicken into thin strips. Cut the veal into
^{3}/$_4$-in (2-cm) pieces; cut the pork slightly smaller.
Arrange the meats on separate platters and lightly salt
the pork, if using; cover and refrigerate. Arrange the
vegetables on a separate platter, cover and refrigerate
until ready to use.
2 Prepare the Mounted Béarnaise Sauce and Achovy
Sauce following the recipes on page 20. Spoon into
individual dipping bowls.
3 Fill a stoneware or metal fondue pot about ^{2}/$_3$ full with
the sherry and add the bouillon cube(s), if using. At the
table, bring the wine just to a rapid simmer. (Alternatively,
measure the required amount, heat on the stove and
transfer to the fondue pot.) Arrange the meat, vegetables
and dipping sauce with the pot on the table.
4 Secure the meat onto wooden skewers, letting the
end of the skewer protrude by ^{1}/$_2$ in (12 mm). Plunge
the meat into the pot for 3–5 minutes (chicken, veal and
pork should not be rare). Repeat with the vegetables,
cooking until desired doneness. Remove from the wine,
drain and dip into individual bowls of sauce, and eat
from the skewers.

Suggested quantities
Vegetables: 6–8 oz (185–250 g) per person (before
trimming)

Serves 4–6

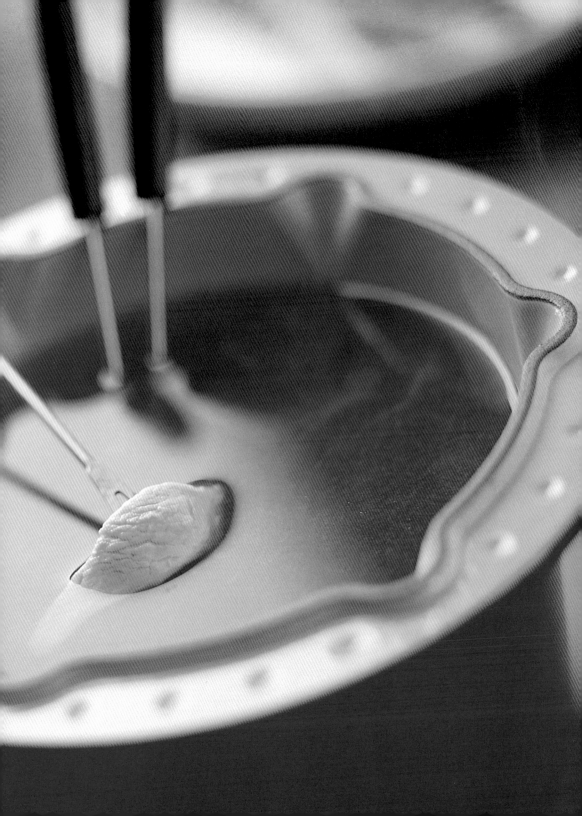

Soy-marinated Beef in Rice Wine

3 lbs (1$^1/_2$ kg) beef flank (skirt) steak, trimmed
Vegetable crudités of choice
3–5 cups (750 ml–1$^1/_4$ liters) rice wine or sake
Curried Mayonnaise (page 21) or other dipping sauces of choice
Steamed rice, green salad and Asian pickles, to serve (optional)

Marinade

1 teaspoon ground ginger
1 teaspoon mustard powder
1 tablespoon molasses or golden syrup
$^1/_2$ cup (125 ml) soy sauce
4 tablespoons peanut oil
3 cloves garlic, finely chopped

Serves 6

1 Thinly slice the beef, cutting across the grain. In a large, shallow bowl, mix all the Marinade ingredients together and toss with the beef. Cover and refrigerate for at least 2 hours or overnight.

2 Prepare the Curried Mayonnaise following the recipe on page 21. Spoon into individual dipping bowls.

3 When ready to serve, drain the marinated meat and arrange it on a serving platter. Arrange the vegetables on a separate serving platter.

4 Fill a stoneware or metal fondue pot $^2/_3$ full with the wine. At the table, heat to a rapid simmer. Arrange the beef, vegetables, dipping sauce and accompaniments with the pot on the table.

5 Secure the meat and vegetables onto skewers, letting the end of each skewer protrude by $^1/_2$ in (12 mm). Plunge each skewer into the pot and cook the strips of meat for 1–2 minutes, and the vegetables for 3–5 minutes. Remove from the wine, drain and dip into individual bowls of sauce and eat with the steamed rice, green salad, and if desired, Asian pickles.

Note: This marinated meat is also excellent fried in a Burgundian fondue (pages 58–61).

Suggested quantities
$^1/_2$–1 cup (50–100 g) cooked rice per person

Spicy Crab and Shrimp Beer Boil

5 lbs (2^1/$_2$ kg) cooked crabs
2^1/$_2$ lbs (1^1/$_4$ kg) jumbo shrimp
  (king prawns)
4 lbs (2 kg) live crawfish (crayfish/
  yabbies) (optional)
Drawn Butter (page 21) and
  seasoned salt, for dipping
Sourdough bread and tossed
  green salad, to serve

Beer Boil

2 teaspoons mustard seed
1 teaspoon coarsely-ground pepper
6 whole cloves
1 teaspoon ground mace (optional)
1 tablespoon paprika
1^1/$_2$ tablespoons dried thyme,
  crumbled
2 teaspoons cayenne pepper, or
  to taste
1 tablespoon fennel seed
2 bay leaves, crumbled
2 tablespoons rock salt, or to taste
1 stalk celery, coarsely chopped or
  2 teaspoons celery seed, ground
1 in (2^1/$_2$ cm) fresh ginger root,
  thinly sliced
4–5 cups (1–1^1/$_4$ liters) lager beer

Serves 6

1 Clean the crab by pulling off the apron flap from under its shell. Pry off the top shell and rinse away the breathing ducts or lungs. Break or cut the body in half, or in larger crabs, cut into smaller pieces. Twist off claws. Arrange the crab parts on a serving platter. If the shrimp still have their heads, twist them off and reserve to add to the beer boil for added flavor; do not shell.

2 Rinse the crawfish in a colander then place in the freezer for 30 minutes until dead. (This also prevents them from splashing hot liquid at the table. Take care when handling the crawfish, as their pincers are sharp. Use tongs, or grab them directly behind the head.) Arrange all the seafood attractively on a serving platter, cover, and refrigerate until required.

3 Prepare the Drawn Butter following the recipe on page 21. Spoon into individual dipping bowls.

4 To make the Beer Boil, combine all the dry seasonings, except the salt, and grind to a powder in a mortar or a spice grinder.

5 Fill a stoneware or nonreactive metal fondue pot about ^{1}/$_2$ full with the Beer Boil and add the ground seasonings, salt, ginger and celery. At the table, bring to a rapid simmer. Arrange the platter of seafood, dipping bowls of sauce and seasoned salt, bread and salad with the pot on the table.

6 Add just enough of the crab to comfortably fit in the pot. Simmer until the flesh is hot, 3–5 minutes. Add the shrimp to the pot and cook until the flesh is firm, about 3 minutes. Add the crawfish and cook until the color changes and the flesh is firm, 3–5 minutes. Supply bibs, finger bowls, hand towels and bowls for the shells. Let guests shell their own shrimp and crawfish, and use fondue forks to extract the crabmeat from the shell. Dip the cooked seafood in the sauce and eat with sourdough bread and tossed green salad.

Note: A clean electric coffee grinder is also excellent for grinding the dry seasonings for this recipe.

Seafood in Court Bouillon

1 lobster tail (optional)

1 lb (500 g) fresh medium shrimp (prawns), shelled (tails left on and shells reserved)

One 10-oz (300-g) jar fresh oysters

One 14-oz (440-g) can abalone (optional)

12 oz (350 g) fresh scallops or squid (calamari) rings

36 fresh small clams, scrubbed

1¹/₂ lbs (750 g) firm white fish fillets such as cod, perch, or halibut, cut into bite-sized pieces

Drawn Butter (page 21) or Quick Ponzu Sauce (page 22), for dipping

Crusty bread, to serve

Court Bouillon

5 cups (1¹/₄ liters) water

Reserved shrimp and lobster shells (above)

Reserved oyster and abalone juice (above)

2 carrots, peeled, coarsely chopped

1 onion, diced

4 sprigs parsley

1 teaspoon dried thyme

2 bay leaves

¹/₂ teaspoon peppercorns

1 teaspoon salt

1 clove garlic, crushed

Pinch of cayenne pepper

1¹/₂ cups (375 ml) white wine

Serves 6

1 If using the lobster, use shears to cut up and along the under-ribs of the shell; pry open and remove the meat from its shell. Reserve the shells for the Court Bouillon and slice the meat into medallions. "Butterfly" the shrimp by slicing deeply lengthwise along the back to remove the vein. Do not cut all the way through. Gently score the underside of the shrimp to prevent curling. Drain the oysters and abalone (if using), reserving their juices for the Court Bouillon. Slice the abalone paper-thin. Arrange all the seafood attractively on a serving platter, cover, and refrigerate until required.

2 Prepare the Drawn Butter or Quick Ponzu Sauce following the recipe on page 21 or 22. Spoon into individual dipping bowls.

3 To prepare the Court Bouillon, combine all the ingredients in a large nonreactive saucepan, cover and bring to a boil. Remove the lid, reduce the heat and simmer for 20 minutes. When ready to serve, strain to discard the shells and transfer to a fondue pot maintaining a gentle simmer, about 325–350 °F (160–175 °C) at the table. The broth should fill ²/₃ of the pot. If not, add boiling water. Arrange the platter of seafood and dipping bowls of sauces with the pot on the table.

4 To serve, use small wire-mesh baskets, skewers, or chopsticks to dip the seafood into the simmering broth. Cook the shrimp for about 3 minutes. The clams are done when open, 2–3 minutes; discard any that do not open. Cook white fish and lobster until white throughout, about 2 minutes.

5 Cook the scallops until just opaque, 1–2 minutes. The squid will take only 1 minute, and the oysters 30 seconds. Add the abalone at the end and cook about 30 seconds to just heat through. Take care not to overcook the seafood, or it will be tough. Remove the cooked seafood from the broth and dip into the sauce. At the end, serve cups of the simmering cooking broth, accompanied with the bread, finger bowls and towels.

Classic Burgundian Fondue

3 lbs (1^1/$_2$ kg) veal loin or beef tenderloin (fillet)

Trimmed parsley sprigs, to garnish

3–5 cups (750 ml–1^1/$_4$ liters) grapeseed or peanut oil, or Clarified Butter (page 24) or ghee, melted, or a combination

Salt and freshly ground white pepper, to taste

Mounted Béarnaise Sauce (page 20) plus other dipping sauces of choice, for dipping

Mushroom or green salad, pickled onions, olives and bread, to serve

Serves 6

1 Cut the meat into ^{3}/$_4$-in (2-cm) cubes and arrange on a serving platter. Garnish with parsley sprigs, cover and refrigerate.

2 Prepare the Clarified Butter (if using) following the recipe on page 24. Prepare the Mounted Béarnaise Sauce following the recipe on page 20, and spoon into individual dipping bowls.

3 Fill a fondue pot no more than ^{1}/$_3$ with the oil, or butter and/or ghee. At the table, heat to 325–350 °F (165–175 °C). Sprinkle the meat with the salt and pepper. Secure the meat onto skewers, letting the end of the skewer protrude by ^{1}/$_2$ in (12 mm). Arrange the platter of meat, dipping bowls of sauces, salad, pickled onions, olives, and bread with the pot of oil on the table.

4 Plunge the meat into the pot and cook until the desired doneness, 2–3 minutes. Remove from the oil, dip in the sauce and eat with the accompaniments. Wait until the oil, butter, or ghee has cooled completely before removing the pot from the table.

Fondue variations

Substitute thin strips of beef flank (skirt) and thread them onto the skewers. Cook for 1 minute. Game meat also works well here, especially venison loin. If desired, rub with a Spice Rub (page 61) first for added flavor or marinate with Aromatic Oil Marinade (page 23). This marinade adds flavor to any tender beef, veal, pork loin, and boneless chicken. Marinate the cubed or diced meat for several hours, then proceed as above.

Beef with a Spice Rub

3 lbs (1$^1/_2$ kg) beef flank (skirt) steak, trimmed
Sprigs of parsley, to garnish
3–5 cups (750 ml–1$^1/_4$ liters) grapeseed or peanut oil
Mounted Béarnaise Sauce (page 20) plus other dipping
   sauces of choice, for dipping

Spice Rub
1 tablespoon juniper berries
1 tablespoon peppercorns
1 teaspoon whole allspice
$^1/_4$ teaspoon ground (powdered) ginger
$^1/_2$ teaspoon mustard powder
2 bay leaves, crumbled
4 tablespoons coarse salt

1 Make the Spice Rub by combining all the ingredients, except the bay leaves and salt, and grind to a coarse powder in a mortar or spice grinder. Stir in the bay leaves and salt. Rub the Spice Rub into the beef, cover and refrigerate for 2–3 hours. When ready to serve, scrape off the seasoning and thinly slice the meat across the grain. Arrange the meat slices on a serving platter and garnish with the parsley.
2 Prepare the Mounted Béarnaise Sauce following the recipe on page 20. Spoon into individual dipping bowls.
3 Pour the oil into a metal fondue pot, filling it no more than $^1/_3$ full. At the table, heat to 325–350 ˚F (165–175 ˚C). Thread the meat on the skewers, letting them protrude by $^1/_2$ in (12 mm). Arrange the platter of meat and dipping bowls of sauces with the pot of oil on the table.
4 Dip the meat in the oil and cook until the desired doneness, about 1 minute. Remove from the pot, dip in the sauce and eat from the skewers. Let the oil cool fully before removing the pot from the table.

Serves 6

Vegetable and Corn Fondue

1 lb (500 g) small new potatoes (chats), scrubbed
1 sweet potato, peeled
2 carrots, peeled
1 parsnip, peeled
1 lb (500 g) winter squash or pumpkin, peeled and
   deseeded
1 rutabaga (Swede), peeled
1 celeriac (celery root), peeled (optional)
4 tablespoons apple cider vinegar
2 fresh ears corn, shucked
3–5 cups (750 ml–1$^1/_4$ liters) Clarified Butter (page 24)
   or ghee, melted
Salt and freshly-ground white pepper, to taste
Mounted Béarnaise Sauce (page 20) plus other dipping
   sauces of choice, for dipping

1 Prepare the Clarified Butter (if using) and Mounted
Béarnaise Sauce following the recipe on pages 20 and 24.
2 In a large pot of salted water, boil the potatoes until
barely tender when skewered, about 10 minutes.
Drain and allow to cool, then cut into thick slices.
3 Cut the sweet potato, carrots, parsnip, squash or
pumpkin, rutabaga, and celeriac into thick slices.
Plunge into a large pot of salted boiling water and add
the vinegar. Cook for 3 minutes after the water returns
to a boil and then drain. Lay the vegetables out on a
large baking sheet to cool. Cut the corn into 1 in (2$^1/_2$ cm)
thick rounds. (The corn does not require precooking.)
4 Fill a metal fondue pot, no more than $^1/_3$ full with
the Clarified Butter or ghee. At the table, heat to
325–350 °F (165–175 °C). Arrange the vegetables and
dipping bowls of sauces with the pot on the table.
5 Secure pieces of the vegetables onto skewers, letting the skewers protrude by $^1/_2$ in (12 mm). Dip the
vegetable in the oil and cook until desired doneness,
3–5 minutes. Remove from the oil, sprinkle with the
salt and pepper, and dip in the dipping sauce. Let the
oil cool fully before removing the pot from the table.

Serves 6

Greek Lamb Fondue

3 lbs (1$^1/_2$ kg) lamb loin or boneless leg, trimmed and
    cut into $^3/_4$-in (2-cm) cubes
4 tablespoons freshly-squeezed lemon juice
$^1/_3$ cup (90 ml) olive oil
2 teaspoons dried oregano
1 teaspoon finely-chopped garlic
1 teaspoon salt
Oregano, to garnish (optional)
3–5 cups (750 ml–1$^1/_4$ liters) grapeseed or peanut oil,
    or Clarified Butter (page 24) or ghee, melted or a
    combination
4 unpeeled cloves garlic
Mounted Béarnaise Sauce (page 20), Anchovy Sauce
    (page 20) and other sauces, for dipping
Slices of crusty (or toasted) bread, to serve

1 Toss the lamb with the lemon juice, olive oil, oregano,
and garlic. Cover and refrigerate for 2–3 hours. Toss in
salt and arrange on a serving platter. If desired, garnish
with fresh oregano.
2 Prepare the Clarified Butter (if using) following the
recipe on page 24. Make the Mounted Béarnaise Sauce
and Anchovy Sauce as instructed on page 20.
3 Fill a metal fondue pot $^1/_3$ full with the oil, Clarified
Butter, ghee, or a combination. Arranged the lamb,
dipping bowls of sauces and bread with the pot on the
table. Heat the oil to 325–350 °F (165–175 °C) and toss
the garlic cloves into the pot to flavor the oil. Remove
with a small wire-mesh basket when they turn brown.
Spread the browned garlic on the bread.
4 Insert skewers into the lamb cubes, letting the skewer
protrude by $^1/_2$ in (12 mm). Plunge them into the pot
and cook until the desired doneness, 2–3 minutes.
Remove from the pot, dip in the sauce and eat with
crusty bread. Let the oil, butter, or ghee cool completely
before removing the pot from the table.

Serves 6

Garlic Shrimp

2 lbs (1 kg) fresh jumbo shrimp or
king prawns (about 36), shelled
and deveined (tails left on)
1 whole bulb garlic
1 teaspoon red chili pepper flakes
$^1/_3$ cup (90 ml) olive oil
4 tablespoons dry white wine
1 teaspoon salt
3–5 cups (750 ml–$1^1/_4$ liters)
Clarified Butter (page 24) or
ghee, melted
Quick Ponzu Sauce (page 22) plus
other dipping sauces of choice
Slices of crusty or toasted bread,
to serve

Serves 4–6

1 Carefully score the underside of each shrimp with
2 or 3 shallow slashes to prevent curling.
2 Separate the cloves from the garlic bulb and peel half
of them; finely chop. Reserve the unpeeled cloves to
flavor the oil. In a bowl, combine the chopped garlic,
pepper flakes, olive oil, wine and salt. Add the shrimp
and toss to coat. Cover and refrigerate for 2–3 hours.
When ready to serve, drain the shrimp. Arrange them
on a platter and bring to the table.
3 Prepare the Clarified Butter following the recipe on
page 24 and the Quick Ponzu Sauce as instructed on
page 22.
4 Fill a metal fondue pot no more than $^1/_3$ full with the
Clarified Butter or ghee and add the unpeeled garlic.
At the table, heat to 325–350 °F (165–175 °C). Arrange
the platter of shrimp, dipping bowls of sauces and
bread with the pot on the table.
5 Skewer a shrimp through each end, letting the skewer
protrude by $^1/_2$ in (12 mm). Plunge the shrimp into the
hot oil and cook until evenly pink, about 2 minutes.
Remove from the oil and drain. Dip in the dipping
sauce before eating it, with or without the bread.
6 After the initial 20 minutes, the garlic cloves will
become lightly golden and soften. Remove them from
the oil and press onto the bread slices. Let the butter
or ghee cool completely before removing the pot from
the table.

Fondue variation
Garlic calamari: If using whole squid, pull the tentacles
and head from the body, and cut away from just in
front of the eyes. Use your fingers to scoop out the
innards and inner spearlike cartilage from the tube.
Rinse well. Keep tentacles whole. Frozen squid tubes
work equally well; thaw and cut into $^1/_2$ in-(12-mm-)
wide rings. Proceed as in the above recipe, cooking for
1 minute.

Ham and Sesame Cubes

1 cup (125 g) sesame seeds, lightly toasted

3 lbs (1$^1/_2$ kg) ham, cut into $^3/_4$-in (2-cm) cubes

3 tablespoons soy sauce

3–5 cups (750 ml–1$^1/_4$ liters) grapeseed or peanut oil, or Clarified Butter (page 24) or ghee, melted or a combination

Quick Chinese Mustard (page 22), for dipping

Ketchup (tomato sauce), chutney, and soy sauce, for dipping

Serves 4–6

1 Prepare the Clarified Butter (if using) following the recipe on page 24 and Quick Chinese Mustard as instructed on page 22.

2 Preheat the oven to 375 °F (190 °C). Pour the sesame seeds onto a rimmed baking sheet and toast in the oven until lightly golden, 7–10 minutes. Shake occasionally to ensure even browning.

3 Toss the ham with the soy sauce and arrange on a platter; sprinkle with 1 tablespoon of the toasted sesame seeds.

4 Fill a metal fondue pot, no more than $^1/_3$ full with the oil, Clarified Butter, or ghee, or a combination. At the table, heat to 325–350 °F (165–175 °C). Arrange the platter of ham, bowls of dipping sauces and the remaining sesame seeds with the pot on the table.

5 Pierce cubes of ham with skewers. Plunge the ham into the hot oil and cook for about 2 minutes. Remove from the pot and drain. Dip into the Quick Chinese Mustard or one of the condiments, then into the remaining sesame seeds. Let the oil, butter or ghee cool completely before removing the pot from the table.

Vinegar-dipped Potatoes

2 lbs (1 kg) unpeeled small new
  potatoes (chats), well scrubbed
1$^{1}/_{2}$ cups (375 ml) apple cider
  vinegar
1 cup (250 ml) peanut or olive oil
$^{1}/_{2}$ cup (125 g) butter
1 large onion, finely chopped
2 teaspoons whole caraway or
  cumin seed
2 teaspoons salt
$^{1}/_{2}$ teaspoon ground white pepper
Grated horseradish, to serve
Anchovy Sauce (page 20),
  Curried Mayonnaise (page 21),
  or sauces of choice, for dipping

Serves 6

1 Prepare the Anchovy Sauce and Curried Mayonnaise following the recipe on pages 20 and 21. Spoon into individual dipping bowls.
2 Cook the potatoes in a large pot of salted boiling water until barely tender when skewered, 8–10 minutes. Drain.
3 Meanwhile, combine all the other ingredients, except the dipping sauce, in a medium saucepan. Bring to a boil, then reduce the heat and simmer for 5 minutes. Transfer to a warmed nonreactive fondue pot and add the potatoes.
4 At the table, simmer the potatoes until tender but not overcooked, about 20 minutes. Prick the potatoes to determine doneness. Remove the potatoes from the pot and serve with the dipping sauces and horseradish.

Note: Unlike other Burgundian fondues, the potatoes are not fried; the large quantity of vinegar flavoring the oil prevents that. Skewer potatoes with fondue forks, and dip into individual bowls of sauce.

Deviled Kidneys and Chicken Livers

2 lbs (1 kg) lamb or calf kidneys
2 tablespoons plus 1 teaspoon salt
4 cups (1 liter) iced water
3 tablespoons freshly-squeezed
  lemon juice
Quick Chinese Mustard (page 22)
1 tablespoon chopped fresh parsley
1 teaspoon coarsely-ground white
  pepper
3–5 cups (750 ml–1$^1/_4$ liters)
  Clarified Butter (page 24) or
  ghee, melted
Boiled rice and salad, to serve

Serves 4–6

1 Prepare the Clarified Butter (if using) and Quick Chinese Mustard following the recipe on page 22 and page 24.
2 Trim the kidneys off all visible fat. Slice in half lengthwise, then use kitchen shears to cut away the white core. Pull away any membrane. Cut calf kidneys into $^3/_4$-in (2-cm) pieces; cut lamb kidneys in half crosswise, creating 2 fat crescents.
3 Dissolve 2 tablespoons of the salt in the water and add 2 tablespoons of the lemon juice. Add the kidneys and soak for 15 minutes. Drain and pat dry with paper towels. Place the kidney pieces in a bowl and add 2 tablespoons of Quick Chinese Mustard, parsley, and the remaining salt and lemon juice; toss to coat evenly. Pierce the kidney pieces onto skewers. Arrange the skewers on a serving platter and sprinkle with the pepper. Cover and refrigerate until ready to serve.
4 Fill a metal fondue pot, no more than $^1/_3$ full with the Clarified Butter or ghee. At the table, heat to 325–350 °F (165–175 °C). Place the kidney and the accompaniments with the pot on the table.
5 Plunge the skewers into the pot and cook for about 3 minutes. Remove the skewers from the pot, dip the cooked kidney pieces in the dipping sauce, and eat with the boiled rice and salad. Let the butter or ghee cool completely before removing the pot from the table.

Fondue variation
Substitute trimmed chicken livers for the kidneys, but do not soak in water. Proceed as above, cooking for 1–2 minutes. If desired, add pitted prunes and dates or water chestnuts to the skewers.

Curried Fish Strips

2 lbs (1 kg) firm white fish fillets, such as cod, floun-
der or halibut
1 cup (125 g) flour
$1/_2$ teaspoon cayenne pepper
2 tablespoons ground red pepper
1 teaspoon salt
3–5 cups (750 ml–$1^1/_4$ liters) grapeseed or peanut oil,
or Clarified Butter (page 24) or ghee, melted
3–6 eggs
Mounted Béarnaise Sauce (page 20), Curried
Mayonnaise (page 21), bottled tartare sauce and/or
soy sauce, for dipping

1 Cut the fish into strips 2 in (5 cm) long, 1 in ($2^1/_2$ cm)
wide, and $1/_2$ in (12 mm) thick. Thread these onto
skewers, letting the end of each skewer protrude by
$1/_2$ in (12 mm).
2 Sift the flour, cayenne, ground red pepper, and salt
into a bowl. Dredge the fish in the seasoned flour.
Place on a tray, with waxed paper between the layers,
and refrigerate up to 6 hours, or until ready to serve.
3 Prepare the Clarified Butter (if using), Mounted
Béarnaise Sauce and Curried Mayonnaise as instructed
on pages 20, 21 and 24. Spoon the dipping sauces into
individual dipping bowls.
4 To serve, arrange the fish on a serving platter. Place
1 egg in each of 6 small, deep bowls, or use 3 bowls
to be shared between 2 people. Lightly beat the eggs.
Fill a metal fondue pot $1/_3$ full with the oil, butter, or
ghee. At the table, heat to 325–350 °F (165–175 °C).
5 Dip the skewers in the beaten egg, drain, and plunge
into the hot oil. Fry until lightly golden, about 2 minutes.
If fish pieces break during cooking, use a small wire-mesh
basket or slotted spoon to retrieve them. Serve with
the dipping sauces alongside.

Note: If the bowls are too shallow, use a pastry brush
to coat skewers with the egg dip.

Serves 6

Shabu Shabu Hot Pot

3 lbs (1$^1/_2$ kg) well-marbled beef tenderloin (fillet) or sirloin
1 lb (500 g) soft tofu, cut into 1-in (2$^1/_2$-cm) cubes, rinsed
1 green onion, cut into 2-in (5-cm) diagonal lengths
Leaves from $^1/_4$ head Chinese napa cabbage
2 carrots, peeled and cut into thin rounds
1 bunch spinach or chrysanthemum leaves, stemmed
8-in (20-cm) piece konbu
1 portion Quick Ponzu Sauce (page 22), for dipping
Steamed rice, to serve

1 Cut the beef wafer-thin across the grain. Arrange the beef slices attractively, slightly overlapping, on a platter or individual plates. Cover and refrigerate until ready to serve. Soak the tofu in fresh water for 20 minutes, then drain. Decoratively arrange the tofu and vegetables on a platter.
2 Prepare the Quick Ponzu Sauce as instructed on page 22. Spoon into individual dipping bowls.
3 Wipe the konbu with a damp cloth to remove any grit. Place it in a Japanese *donabe* or fondue pot (if using a coal firepot, see pages 14–15 for instructions). Fill the pot $^2/_3$ full with cold water. At the table, bring to a rapid simmer and remove the kelp. Maintain the stock at a rapid simmer. Arrange the meat, vegetables, bowls of dipping sauce and steamed rice around the pot on the table.
4 To cook the meat, use chopsticks or fondue forks to "swish" pieces of meat in the stock to the desired doneness, about 10 seconds. Place the vegetable pieces in the stock until the desired doneness, 2–5 minutes. Retrieve the vegetables using small wire-mesh baskets. Dip the cooked food in the dipping sauce and eat with the steamed rice.

Serves 6

Chicken Mizutaki Firepot

3 lbs (1$^1/_2$ kg) boneless, skinless chicken thighs and breasts, cut into bite-sized pieces
20 dried black (shiitake) mushrooms
$^1/_2$ green onion
1 bunch asparagus, trimmed
1 green bell pepper (capsicum), deseeded
Leaves from $^1/_4$ head Chinese napa cabbage
2 carrots, peeled and cut into thin disks
$^1/_4$ cauliflower, broken into small florets, stems peeled and sliced
1 head broccoli, broken into small florets, stems peeled and sliced
4–6 cups (1–1$^1/_2$ liters) Chicken Broth (page 25)
Mizutaki Sauce (page 24) or Quick Ponzu Sauce (page 22), for dipping
Steamed rice, to serve

Serves 6

1 Place the chicken pieces in a sieve. Pour boiling water over them and drain. Allow to cool. Arrange the pieces on a serving platter, cover and refrigerate until ready to serve.

2 Soak the mushrooms in warm water until soft, about 30 minutes. Drain. Use scissors to snip off the tough stems; discard. Cut the green onion and asparagus into 2-in (5-cm) lengths. Cut the bell pepper into 2 in (5 cm) long sticks. Arrange the vegetables in groups attractively on a platter and cover; refrigerate until ready to serve.

3 Prepare the Quick Ponzu Sauce or Mizutaki Sauce as instructed on page 22 or 24. Spoon into individual dipping bowls.

4 To serve, pour the Chicken Broth into a Japanese *donabe* or a fondue pot, filling it about $^2/_3$ full. (If using a coal firepot, refer to pages 14–15 for instructions.) Arrange the chicken pieces, vegetables and dipping sauces around the pot of broth on the table. Bring the Chicken Broth to a rapid simmer. Add the vegetables as desired, retrieving loose vegetable pieces with a small wire-mesh basket.

5 Use chopsticks to dip pieces of the chicken in the broth and cook until done, no less than 3 minutes. Dip the cooked food in the dipping sauce and eat with steamed rice. When finished, ladle the broth into the rice bowls.

Note: Both Shabu Shabu and Chicken Mizutaki are *nabemono*, Japanese one-pot dishes cooked at the table. The dipping sauces served with them may be garnished with salt, sesame seeds, and a pinch of cayenne or *sansho* (Japanese pepper). Accompany with assorted tart pickled vegetables, particularly Japanese *tsukemono*.

Korean Firepot

1 1/2 lbs (750 g) boneless beef
  shank (leg shin), trimmed
6 hard-boiled eggs, shelled
4 cups (1 liter) Enriched Meat
  Stock (Page 25)
Steamed rice, to serve
Kimchi, to serve
1 portion Korean Vinegar Dipping
  Sauce (page 24), for dipping

Marinade
2 tablespoons sesame seeds,
  lightly toasted (page 69)
1/2 cup (125 ml) soy sauce
2 tablespoons rice vinegar or
  distilled white vinegar
3 tablespoons peanut oil, preferably
  cold-pressed
1 clove garlic, crushed

Meatballs
1 lb (500 g) ground (minced) pork
2 tablespoons pine nuts
1/2 cup (60 g) cornstarch (cornflour)
2 eggs, lightly beaten
2–4 tablespoons oil

Vegetables
10 oz (300 g) button mushrooms
1 daikon radish or 2 turnips, peeled
3 carrots, peeled
2 stalks celery
Leaves from 1/4 head Chinese
  napa cabbage, quartered
1/2 green onion, cut into 2-in
  (5-cm) lengths

Serves 6

1 Prepare the Marinade by crushing the sesame seeds in a mortar, then stir in all the other ingredients. Reserve 4 tablespoons of the Marinade for the pork. Slice the beef as thinly as possible, then cut into matchsticks (thin cuts are important, as this beef is chewy). Toss the slices in the Marinade and set aside.

2 To prepare the Meatballs, use your hands to blend the reserved Marinade into the ground pork. Knead for several minutes, as this helps to create a firm texture. Pinch off a small ball and place a pine nut in its center. Using hands to prevent sticking, form into a ball. Continue until all the meat and nuts are used up. You should have about 50 meatballs. Place the meatballs on a rimmed baking sheet and sieve the cornstarch over; shake the tray to coat the meatballs. Brush off any excess cornstarch. Dip each meatball into the beaten egg. In a skillet over medium heat, heat the oil and brown the meat on all sides until cooked through, about 5 minutes. Set aside. You may need to do this in 2 batches; if so, use additional oil.

3 To prepare the Vegetables, wipe the mushrooms with a damp cloth to remove grit. If the mushrooms are large, slice in half. Cut the daikon or turnips into strips of 1/8 in (3 mm) thick and 2 in (5 cm) long; do the same with the carrots. Cut the celery stalks into 2-in (5-cm) long pieces, then slice the pieces into thin sticks.

4 Prepare the Enriched Meat Stock and Korean Vinegar Dipping Sauce as instructed on pages 24 and 25.

5 Arrange the vegetables, meats and whole eggs by group, attractively in a firepot or metal fondue pot. (If using a coal firepot, refer to pages 14–15 for instructions.) Fill the pot with enough stock to the rim, but do not overfill. At the table, bring to a rapid simmer. (Alternatively, bring the stock to a boil on the stove and pour into the pot.) Cook to the desired doneness, about 5 minutes. Use small wire-mesh baskets and chopsticks to transfer food from the pot to individual bowls of steamed rice. Accompany with dipping sauce and kimchi.

Coconut and Seafood Hot Pot

Juice from 3 limes

Drawn Butter (page 21) and Nuoc
  Cham Dipping Sauce (page 22),
  for dipping

Seafood Platter

2 lbs (1 kg) fresh jumbo shrimp
  (king prawns)

$3/4$ lb (375 g) fresh scallops or
  squid (calamari) rings

One 10-oz (300-g) jar oysters

$1^1/_2$ lbs (750 g) firm white fish fillets

Vegetable Platter

1 cucumber, peeled, halved
  lengthwise and sliced

1 green onion, cut into
  2-in (5-cm) lengths

8 oz (250 g) green beans, cut into
  2-in (5-cm) lengths

3 cups (150 g) bean sprouts

1 bunch fresh cilantro (coriander
  leaves), coarsely chopped

Broth

1 tablespoon oil

6 Asian shallots, coarsely chopped

2 cloves garlic, crushed

$1/_2$ in (12 mm) fresh galangal or
  ginger root, peeled and sliced

1 teaspoon red pepper flakes

1 tablespoon salt

2 teaspoons sugar

4 cups (1 liter) water, or more as
  needed

$1^1/_2$ cups (375 ml) thin coconut
  cream or thick coconut milk

2 stalks lemongrass, thick bottom
  part only, outer layers discarded

1 To prepare the Seafood Platter, remove the shrimp heads and shells, but keep the tails intact. If using raw shrimp, "butterfly" the shrimp by slicing deeply lengthwise along the back to remove the vein. Do not cut all the way through. Gently score the underside of the shrimp to prevent curling. If the scallops still have their roe, retain, but cut away the black vein around the scallop. Drain the oysters, adding their liquid to the Court Bouillon. Remove all the skin and bones from the fish fillets and cut into bite-sized pieces. Arrange the seafood attractively on a platter, cover and refrigerate until ready to serve.

2 To prepare the Vegetable Platter, arrange all the vegetables on a platter and sprinkle generously with the cilantro, cover and refrigerate until ready to serve.

3 Prepare the Drawn Butter and Nuoc Cham Dipping Sauce as instructed on pages 21 and 22.

4 Prepare the Broth by heating the oil over medium heat. Sauté the shallots and garlic until golden, 2–3 minutes. Add all the other ingredients except the lime juice and bring to a rapid simmer. Transfer to the firepot or a stoneware or metal fondue pot, filling it $2/_3$ full. If necessary, add boiling water.

5 To serve, add the lime juice to the pot and bring the Broth to a rapid simmer at the table. Drop individual pieces of the vegetable into the simmering Broth and cook until the desired doneness, about 2 minutes for the cucumber, bean sprouts and green onion, and up to 5 minutes for the beans. Use small wire-mesh baskets or skewers to secure each piece of shellfish and cook till just done. Precooked seafood merely requires heating through, while raw shellfish a few minutes: 3 minutes for shrimp, 1–2 minutes for scallops and 1 minute for squid. Do not overcook the seafood. Remove from the Broth and eat as it is or dipped into the dipping sauce.

6 Spoon the Broth into individual soup bowls (**Note**: the ginger and lemongrass are not eaten) and if desired, season with Nuoc Cham Dipping Sauce or fish sauce.

Serves 6

Vietnamese Lau

2 packets (40 sheets) rice paper
  wrappers
1 cup (150 g) peanuts (ground
  nuts), crushed, to serve
1 portion Nuoc Cham Dipping
  Sauce (page 22), for dipping

Beef Platters
1 onion, thinly sliced
1 tablespoon rice vinegar or
  distilled white vinegar
3 lbs (1^1/$_2$ kg) beef sirloin or
  tenderloin (fillet), trimmed and
  cut into paper-thin slices
2 tablespoons sesame oil
2 teaspoons ground white pepper

Vegetable Platters
Leaves from 3 heads butter
  (Boston) lettuce
1 cucumber, peeled, halved
  lengthwise and thinly sliced
1 green onion, cut into
  2-in (5-cm) lengths
3 cups (150 g) bean sprouts
Sprigs from 1 bunch fresh mint
1 bunch fresh cilantro (coriander
  leaves)
1 bunch Thai or sweet basil

Broth
2 tablespoons oil
2 cloves garlic, thinly sliced
1 in (2^1/$_2$ cm) fresh ginger root,
  thinly sliced
1 stalk lemongrass, thick bottom
  part only, outer layers discarded,
  inner part sliced (optional)
1 cup (250 ml) rice vinegar or
  distilled white vinegar
5 cups (1^1/$_4$ liters) water
1 tablespoon salt
3 tablespoons sugar

1 Cover the rice paper wrappers with a damp cloth until needed. About 1 hour before the meal, dip each rice paper in warm water for 10 seconds to soften. Stack, interspersing each rice paper with well-moistened waxed paper, and wrap the stack in plastic wrap to prevent drying. Should they stick together, brush liberally with water at the table.

2 To prepare the Beef Platters, toss the onion slices with the vinegar in a small bowl. Arrange the beef slices attractively on 2 platters, overlapping as little as possible. Drizzle with a little oil and sprinkle with pepper. Drain the onion slices, discarding the vinegar, and break into rings. Place decoratively over the meat. Cover and refrigerate until ready to serve.

3 To prepare the Vegetable Platters, tear any large lettuce leaves in half, and cut away the stiff cores. Arrange all the vegetables in groups on a platter. Cover and refrigerate until ready to serve.

4 To make the Broth, heat the oil over medium heat in a large saucepan. Add the garlic and ginger, and sauté until fragrant, 1–2 minutes. Add all the other ingredients and bring to a rapid simmer. Strain the Broth into a hot pot or metal fondue pot. The broth should fill the pot about ^{2}/$_3$ full; if not, add boiling water to the desired depth. (If using a coal firepot, refer to pages 14–15 for instructions.)

5 To serve, arrange the rice paper wrappers, Beef Platters, Vegetables Platters and condiments around the pot on the table. Bring the Broth to a rapid simmer. Invite your guests to lay a sheet of softened rice paper on a plate and center a lettuce leaf, a few herb sprigs, and some marinated onions from the meat platter. Drop a piece of meat into the simmering Broth until the desired doneness, about 10 seconds. Retrieve with chopsticks or a wire-mesh basket and lay the cooked meat over the vegetables. If desired, sprinkle with ground peanuts, then fold to enclose the bottom and top, and roll up. Dip the roll in the dipping sauce and eat with fingers.

Serves 6

Mongolian Firepot

4–6 cups (1–1$\frac{1}{2}$ liters) Enriched
Meat Stock (page 25)
2 tablespoons rice wine or dry
sherry
1 portion Mongolian Firepot Dip
(page 23)
Condiments of choice, such as
plum sauce, hoisin sauce,
and satay sauce
6 eggs (optional)
4 oz (125 g) dried cellophane
noodles (glass noodles)

Meat Platters
12 oz (350 g) flank steak
(skirt steak)
12 oz (350 g) boneless lean lamb,
such as loin
4 boneless, skinless chicken
breast halves, thinly sliced
2 tablespoons soy sauce
2 tablespoons sesame oil
$\frac{1}{2}$ in (12 mm) fresh ginger root,
grated
1 small clove garlic, crushed

Vegetable Platters
1 lb (500 g) soft tofu, cut into
$\frac{3}{4}$-in (2-cm) cubes
2 turnips or 1 rutabaga, peeled
Leaves from $\frac{1}{2}$ head Chinese
napa cabbage
$\frac{1}{2}$ bunch spinach, stemmed
4 oz (125 g) fresh mushrooms
4 oz (125 g) snow peas, trimmed
1 green onion, cut into
2-in (5-cm) lengths

1 Prepare the Meat Platters by cutting the beef and lamb into paper-thin slices. Lay the meat slices slightly overlapping on separate platters. In a bowl, combine the soy sauce, sesame oil, ginger and garlic. Add the chicken slices and toss to coat. Arrange the chicken on a separate platter. Wrap and refrigerate the meat and chicken until ready to serve.

2 Meanwhile, prepare the Vegetable Platters. Soak the tofu in water for 20 minutes, then drain. Halve any large mushrooms. Cut the turnips or rutabaga into thin strips about 2 in (5 cm) long. Arrange all the vegetables decoratively on a serving platter or plates.

3 Prepare the Mongolian Firepot Dip and Enriched Meat Stock following the recipe on pages 23 and 25.

4 To serve, add the Enriched Meat Stock and wine to a firepot or a metal fondue pot. (If using a coal firepot, refer to pages 14–15 for instructions.) Arrange the Meat Platters, Vegetable Platters and accompaniments around the pot of broth on the table. Bring the broth to a rapid simmer.

5 At the table, have guests individually cook their meats and vegetables to desired doneness, using small wire ladles, chopsticks or skewers. Meats will cook between 10 to no more than 20 seconds, depending on the thickness and desired doneness. Spinach cooks within 10 seconds, but other vegetables may take 2 minutes or longer. Serve the dipping sauce and condiments alongside. If desired, break an egg into individual small bowls, beat lightly, and serve as a second dipping sauce.

6 Midway through the meal, soak the noodles in hot water for 10 minutes; drain and set aside. When guests have finished the meat and vegetables, add the noodles to the cooking stock. Ladle bowls of broth and noodles for each diner.

Serves 6 to 8

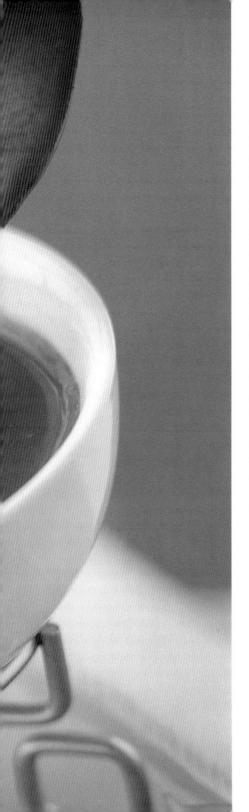

Classic Chocolate Fondue

$^1/_2$ cup (125 ml) cream
2 tablespoons kirsch, triple sec or brandy
9 oz (280 g) milk chocolate, preferably Swiss, chopped
Fruits including: dried pineapple, mango and apple;
   fresh pears, strawberries, tangerine or mandarin slices
Ladyfingers and profiteroles

In a double boiler over simmering water, heat the cream and liqueur or brandy. Add the chocolate all at once and stir until smooth. Transfer to a warmed stoneware or metal fondue pot, and accompany with the fruits. Skewer pieces of fruit on fondue forks and dip in the chocolate sauce. Remove and eat. Dip the ladyfingers or profiteroles in the sauce by hand.

Note: The original chocolate fondue was created in New York by a publicist for Toblerone chocolate. If desired, substitute Toblerone milk chocolate. Its bits of slightly melted honey and almond nougat enhance the flavor.

Suggested quantities
Fruits: about 2-4 oz (60-125 g) per person
Cookies (biscuits): about 4 per person

Serves 6

Candied Ginger and Dark Chocolate Fondue

One 12-oz (375-g) jar candied ginger in syrup (see note)
4 tablespoons evaporated milk
1–2 tablespoons rum
6 oz (175 g) semisweet (plain) chocolate, chopped
Fruits including: crystallized ginger pieces, candied
   (glacéed) and fresh cherries, dried pineapple, mango
   and papaya, glazed apricots, cut into thick strips,
   dates, hulled strawberries, and pear slices

1 Drain the ginger and reserve the liquid. (If it has totally
crystallized, place it in a pan of warm water over low
heat until melted, or in a microwave for 10 seconds.)
Reserve the ginger pieces for later use.
2 In a double boiler over simmering water, combine the
ginger syrup, milk, rum and chocolate. Stir until melted.
Transfer to a warmed stoneware or metal fondue pot.
Skewer pieces of ginger or fruit on fondue forks and
dip in the chocolate sauce. Remove and eat.

Note: Candied ginger in syrup is available at Asian
supermarkets, often in decorative pottery jars. If
unavailable, use crystallized ginger and add $1/2$ teaspoon ground (powdered) ginger to the chocolate.

Suggested quantities
Fruits: about 2-4 oz (60-125 g) per person
Cookies (biscuits): about 4 per person

Serves 4

Rocky Road Fondue

9 oz (280 g) milk chocolate, chopped

$^1/_2$ cup (125 ml) sweetened condensed milk

$^1/_2$ cup (125 ml) cream

1 tablespoon brewed coffee

1 tablespoon rum (optional)

8 oz (250 g) large marshmallows

$^1/_2$ cup (75 g) unsalted mixed nuts, lightly toasted and finely ground

Pitted dates, ladyfingers, and cookies (biscuits), to serve

Serves 6

1 In a double boiler over simmering water, combine the chocolate, milk, cream, coffee and rum (if using), and stir until melted. Transfer to a warm fondue pot. Take $^1/_2$ of the marshmallows and cut each in half, reserving the remaining whole marshmallows for the serving platter.

2 At the table, briefly stir the cut marshmallows and all of the nuts into the melted chocolate. Serve the remaining marshmallows on a platter, along with the dates and cookies. Skewer them on fondue forks and dip into the chocolate sauce. Remove and eat.

Note: To toast nuts, preheat the oven to 375 °F (190 °C). Spread the nuts on a rimmed baking sheet and bake until lightly browned, 8–12 minutes.

Suggested quantities
Fruits: about 2-4 oz (60-125 g) per person
Cookies (biscuits): about 4 per person

White Chocolate and Coconut Fondue

$^1/_2$ cup (125 ml) sweetened
  condensed milk
2 tablespoons triple sec
$^1/_2$ cup (125 ml) thick coconut
  cream
8 oz (250 g) white chocolate,
  chopped
Pinch of ground cinnamon
1 tablespoon dried grated (desiccated) coconut
Tropical fruits including: fresh
  pineapple, mango, papaya,
  strawberries and lychees, cut
  into bite-sized chunks
Cookies (biscuits) such as
  coconut macaroons

In a double boiler over simmering water, heat the milk,
liqueur and coconut cream. Add the chocolate all at
once, stirring until melted. Transfer to a warmed
stoneware or metal fondue pot and sprinkle with the
cinnamon and desiccated coconut. Skewer pieces of
fruit on fondue forks and dip in the chocolate sauce.
Remove and eat. Dip macaroons in the sauce by hand.

Suggested quantities
Fruits: about 2-4 oz (60-125 g) per person
Cookies (biscuits): about 4 per person

Serves 6

Butterscotch Fondue

4 tablespoons (60 g) unsalted
  butter
$^2/_3$ cup (150 ml) light corn syrup
$1^1/_4$ cups (9 oz/280 g) firmly
  packed light brown sugar
$^2/_3$ cup (150 ml) cream
1 teaspoon vanilla extract (essence)
Fruits and cookies (biscuits)
  of choice

Serves 4

In a medium saucepan, melt the butter over medium heat. Add the corn syrup and brown sugar, stirring until just dissolved. Bring the mixture to a boil and cook for 2 to 3 minutes. Remove from the heat, then slowly stir in the cream and vanilla. Transfer to a warm fondue pot, and serve with fruit and cookies.

Suggested quantities
Fruits: about 2-4 oz (60-125 g) per person
Cookies (biscuits): about 4 per person

Complete List of Recipes